TALKS
FOR
TOTS

TALKS FOR TOTS

Suggested Stories and Poems
for Short Inspirational Talks

by

Joyce Bowen Maughan

Vol. I

Published by
Deseret Book Company
Salt Lake City, Utah
1975

Copyright 1964
by
Deseret Book Company
Sixth Printing 1975
ISBN 87747-289-0

Printed by

In the United States of America

DEDICATION

To our children:
- JoDean
- LaRee
- Randon
- Teresa
- Melanie
- Kristine.

It was to meet their needs that this book was developed.

ABOUT THE AUTHOR

Joyce Bowen Maughan's training and experience have prepared her to write this book for children.

She received her B.S. Degree at the University of Idaho and has done graduate work at the University of Idaho, Eastern Washington College, and Arizona State University.

Her five years' teaching experience was with the young children in the primary grades of Spokane, Wash. Public Schools. She has served in the Church auxiliaries in many capacities. Two articles concerning her work on the Nampa Stake Sunday School Board appeared in the *Instructor*.

Mrs. Maughan is married to Dean L. Maughan and they are the parents of six children ranging in age from thirteen to one year. Her husband filled a Danish Mission and has served in various bishoprics most of their married life, and also as a high councilman.

They lived for over a year on the Navajo Indian Reservation where her husband taught in a Bureau of Indian Affairs school for Navajo children. While there, they developed a Navajo Teaching Kit of visual aids to be used in teaching about the Navajo people.

Mesa, Arizona is their present home.

FOREWORD

The purpose of this book is to be a guide and reference for parents, teachers, and children in preparing short inspirational talks for the Jr. Sunday School. Many children will assume responsibility for their own talks with a reference book such as this available. They will grow in confidence, knowing that they can "give a talk." It is the author's opinion that a book of this nature will not stifle the young child's creative development, but to the contrary; he will gain confidence in his ability and then delight in creating his own talks once he has learned the pattern.

This book is written with a controlled vocabulary. First grade children will be able to read some of the easier poems. Second grade children will be able to read many selections. Most third grade children will be able to read the entire book without help except for perhaps one or two words in some stories. The number of new words is limited in each story so that the child will not become frustrated. There is a wide range of difficulty. From very, very simple selections for the 4-6 year olds to more difficult items for the 7-9 year olds.

Subject material has been chosen which is within the interest, understanding, and ability of the child from four to nine years of age.

In organizing this book, the author has relied heavily upon her training and experience as an elementary teacher in public school as well as her experience in the organizations of the Church.

Please remember that these stories are for children. If the doctrine presented were developed with all the ramifications, they would be much too difficult for the children they are intended for. The purpose of the book would be lost. These principles of the gospel are stated as simply as possible, in order to make them understandable to the young children of the Church. It is not easy to make Church doctrine understandable to the child from four to eight years of age.

The material is all compatible with the doctrine of The Church of Jesus Christ of Latter-day Saints. It is with a sincere desire to aid the development of our Mormon children that this book has been written and made available.

Joyce B. Maughan

SUGGESTIONS TO THE PARENTS FOR THE USE OF THIS BOOK

So your little one has been asked to give a short inspirational talk in Jr. Sunday School, and you don't know how to begin. This book is designed to help you. There are over one hundred ideas for you.

Young children have the ability and are usually interested in participating in the religious service. It's the parents' responsibility to see that the experience is adapted to the child's age level and abilities. Keep his first experiences simple. Make it easy for him to feel success. The difficulty may increase with his ability and confidence. A short poem is perhaps best for the pre-school child. Older children might use a story. Select material which has only one or two new words for the child. Make certain that these new words are not too difficult and that he can master them. Stumbling over difficult words will cause the child to lose confidence.

If possible, the small child should memorize

his talk. Memorizing gives the child assurance and it will later help him to think on his feet.

Permitting a child to go before an audience unprepared is to teach him carelessness. Notes or a copy in his hand might give him self-confidence; but the material should be known well enough that the child doesn't rely on notes in the practice sessions at home. Don't write his notes for him in cursive writing. He most likely cannot read them. If he does read and write, he might be able to print the notes himself; but they should be printed. The better thing would be to type them on an index card.

It is better to have two short practice sessions each day for six days than to have fifteen or twenty sessions in one or two days. Don't work too hard in one or two sessions, or the child may become frustrated.

After he has mastered the material content, practice to improve the delivery. Remind him to speak to the back of the room so that he will be heard by all. Usually children want to speak too fast. If they will slow down, their speech will be more clear and distinct. If the staring eyes bother him, tell him to look at the foreheads of his audience. Please don't make the practice sessions on the adult level. Remember that the talk must be adapted to his age level and abilities if he is to feel success.

Normally we don't have a small child give the name of the talk nor author credits.

We need to help the child with the ending or he will become upset and not have the good feeling that he should have when completing his assignment.

"A proper ending for a 2½ minute inspirational talk would be a hope and a prayer such as, 'I pray this in the name of Jesus Christ. Amen'; or, 'This is my prayer in the name of Jesus Christ. Amen'."*

The following is a sample of a "talk for a preschool child."

God takes care of little birdies
In the cold and snow
God takes care of little children
Everyday we know! I say this in the name of
    Jesus Christ. Amen.

In this book are included many poems. They make good talks for tots for poetry consists of the "best words in the best order." Poetry is the highest form of literature. Children like poetry. They are hungry for rhymes and repetitions of lovely

---
The Instructor, March 1963, pp. 99.

sounds. This is why the nursery rhymes have endured, while having little thought which the young child understands. Children will often choose a poem for their talk and memorize it easily.

Parents should remember the child's limited ability and not show disappointment if the child has difficulty in his presentation. It is no reflection upon the parent if the child gives less than a professional delivery. The parents' reputation is *not* at stake. The child will do his best, we may be sure. Let him know that you are pleased with him and proud of him being "big enough to talk in Church." Finding fault or pointing out his errors after a talk will only lessen his self-confidence. The next assignment will be a chance for you to work on the weaknesses with a positive approach.

You are helping to prepare a child to become a "servant of God." Be humble and prayerful. All will be well.

In Summary:

1. *Keep it simple* and make it easy for him to feel success.
2. *Practice in many short sessions.* Don't expect a "grown-up" delivery, but he should *know the material.* If he can't learn it—it's too difficult.

3. *Speak to the last one* in the audience and *speak slowly.*
4. *Don't give the name of talk* nor author credits.
5. *End the talk with,*
    I pray this in the name of Jesus Christ, Amen, or This is my prayer in the name of Jesus Christ, Amen.
6. "My, you did well! Daddy and I are so pleased that you were able to talk in Church. I'm sure your Heavenly Father is pleased too."

ACKNOWLEDGMENTS

The author and publisher of TALKS FOR TOTS gratefully acknowledge the courtesy of the following publishers and authors for permission to use copyrighted stories and poems. Some poems are traditional, with the author unknown.

American Book Company: "A Song of Thanks" from *First Year Music* by Hollis Dann.

The Church of Jesus Christ of Latter-day Saints for poems from *The Children Sing* as listed:

"I Think When I Read That Sweet Story," by Jemima Luke
"The Golden Plates," by Rose Thomas Graham
"An Angel Came," by Rose Thomas Graham
"Baptism," by Wallace F. Bennett
"My Body is a Temple," by Esther H. Doolittle
"God Our Father Made the Night," Author Unknown
"Father up Above," by Mabel Jones Gabbott
"God's Daily Care," by Marie C. Turk
"Jesus is our Loving Friend," by Anna Johnson
"Thanks to Our Father," Author Unknown
"I Thank Thee, Dear Father," by George Careless
"For the Beauty of the Earth," by Folliott S. Pierpoint
"Mother Dear," by Maude Belnap Kimball
"Happiness," by Mr. and Mrs. N. W. Christiansen
"Little Lambs so White and Fair," Author Unknown
"I Have Two Little Hands," by Bertha A. Kleinmann
"Let's Be Kind to One Another," by Evan Stephens

Exposition Press Inc.: "Little Things," by Julia A. F. Carney from *Little Things*.

Ginn and Company: "Loving Care" by Nellie Poorman, from *Tuning Up* of *The World of Music series*.

The Instructor Magazine:

"Prayer Answered," by Catherine Bowles, (adapted).

"Testimony," by President George Albert Smith.

"Resolutions," (author unknown).

"Behold Thy Mother," by Mothers' Day Program Committee for 1956.

"Ten Commandments of Reverence," by May Spencer.

Orleans, Mrs. Frieda K., Executrix, Estate of Ilo Orleans, for "Thanksgiving" by Ilo Orleans.

The Reader's Digest Assn., Inc. for "It's Plain Thievery!" by Constance Cameron.

Summy-Birchard Company: "Mother's Day," by Stephen Fay.

TABLE OF CONTENTS

THE BIBLE

In The Beginning	23
Noah	24
Abraham	26
Faith and Obedience of Abraham	27
Joseph	29
The Baby Moses	30
Moses the Deliverer	31
Thou Shalt Have No Other Gods	32
Thou Shalt Not Make Any Graven Image	33
Thou Shalt Not Take The Name of God in Vain	34
Remember the Sabbath Day	35
Honor Thy Father and Thy Mother	36
Thou Shalt Not Kill	38
Thou Shalt Not Steal	39
Thou Shalt Not Bear False Witness	40
Thou Shalt Not Covet	41
The Israelites' Lack of Faith	42
Shadrach, Meshach, and Abed-nego	43
Daniel in the Lion's Den	44
I Think When I Read That Sweet Story	45
Jesus Among the Doctors in the Temple	46
The Baptism of Jesus	47
Jesus Stopped the Storm	48
Jesus Heals the Blind	49
Faith	50
The Temptation of Jesus	51
Let the Little Children Come	52
The Good Samaritan	53
Feeding the 5000	54

THE CHURCH
Going to Church	59
Ten Commandments of Reverence	60
The Golden Plates	62
An Angel Came	63
The Prophet Joseph Smith	64
The Restored Church of Jesus Christ	65
The Church of Jesus Christ of L.D.S.	67
Our Prophet	69
The Kingdom of God	70
How to Get to Heaven	71

THE GOSPEL
Repentance	75
A Road Map for Life	76
Sin and Faith	77
Baptism	78
I Want to be Baptized	79
Baptism	80
The Holy Ghost	81
The Holy Ghost	82
Prayer	83
Prayer	84
Prayer	85
Prayer Answered	86
My Tithing Gives Me Happiness	87
The Law of Tithing and Jacob	88
My Body	89
Our Engine—the Body	90
Keeping the Word of Wisdom	91
My Body is a Temple	93
Do Not Be Deceived	94
Freedom in the Church	95

HOME AND FAMILY
Family	99
Family	100

Only One Mother 101
A Home of Loving Deeds 102
Kind Actions 103
Do What's Right 104

PRAISING GOD
Jesus, The Son of God 107
Thanks to our Father 108
For Health and Food 108
Dear Lord 109
My Soul is Thine 110
We Thank Thee 112
God Our Father Made the Night 113
Father, We Thank Thee for the Night 114
Father Up Above 115
Loving Care 116
God's Daily Care 117
Jesus is our Loving Friend 118
Thanks to our Father 119
Father, Thou Who Carest 120
I Thank Thee, Dear Father 121
Little Things 122

SEASONAL AND SPECIAL OCCASIONS
Resolutions 125
Easter 126
He is Risen 127
For the Beauty of the Earth 128
Mother's Day 129
Mother Dear 130
Honor Thy Mother 131
Father's Day 133
A Song of Thanks 134
Thanksgiving 135
My Gift 137
Christmas Night 138
The Birth of Christ 139

Tidings of Great Joy 140
The Wise Men 141

STRENGTH OF CHARACTER
Honesty 145
The Long and Short of It 146
Dear God 147
Setting a Goal 148
Happiness 149
He Didn't Give Up 150
Try, Try Again 151
Fight for the Right 152
Charting a Course 153
Road Signs 154
Obedience 155
Obedience 156
Little Lambs so White and Fair 157
I Have Two Little Hands 158
Gravity 159
Stuck 160
Let's Be Kind to One Another 161
It's Plain Thievery! 163
A Healthy Spirit 164
A New Hobby 165
The Lord is My Shepherd 166

The Bible

(Also, see Seasonal and Special Occasions.)

IN THE BEGINNING

Long before we were born on this earth we lived as spirit children with God, our Heavenly Father, and our brother, Jesus Christ. We were happy and we loved one another.

We needed bodies as we have on this earth; so God made this earth. He put Adam and Eve on it. Adam and Eve became the first parents. They are great-great-great-grandparents to all the people on earth.

If we live as our Heavenly Father wants us to, we will be able to live with him again. We will know Jesus. We will be with our families.

NOAH
from the Bible

Many, many years ago, the people on the earth were very bad. They were so bad that God was sorry that he had made them. He decided to destroy them.

A man named Noah was a good man. God wanted to save him. He told Noah how to build a big boat, called an Ark. When the Ark was finished, God told Noah to take his family on it. He took some of all the different animals, too. There was food for all. This was as God commanded. Then it started to rain. For forty days and forty nights it rained. All the living things on the earth were drowned. Noah and everything in the Ark were safe.

When the water was gone, Noah and his family went out of the Ark on to dry land. All of the animals went out of the Ark and found new homes.

Noah built an altar and offered thanks for their many blessings. Our Heavenly Father placed a rainbow in the sky as a sign of his promise that he would never again send another flood over the whole earth. When we see a rainbow, we think of Noah and remember that he did as God commanded.

If we do as our Heavenly Father commands, we will be blessed.

ABRAHAM
from the Bible

Abraham lived a long time ago. He was a good man. The people where he lived did not worship God as Abraham did. Because Abraham worshiped God as he knew he should, God talked with him. He told Abraham to go to a land which God had chosen for him. God promised Abraham that he would bless him and make him great. All the families on earth would be blessed through Abraham.

Abraham moved his wife, his family, his servants, and all they owned to the new land. They found it a choice land. It was a beautiful land. Soon Abraham had many cattle and sheep. They were grateful that God had sent them to this new land. Abraham built a place to pray called an altar. He thanked God for his blessings.

If we are good and worship God as we should, God will bless us, too.

THE FAITH AND OBEDIENCE OF ABRAHAM
from the Bible, Genesis 22:1-18

Abraham was often tested by the Lord. One test was more difficult than the rest. Abraham was commanded to offer Isaac, his son as a sacrifice on an altar.

It was the practice in those days to offer the best animals on an altar. This was to remind the people of the great sacrifice which our Heavenly Father would make when he would offer his Son, Jesus Christ, to save mankind.

Abraham made ready to do as he was commanded. He tied the son he loved so dearly, placed him on the altar, and lifted the knife.

Just then an angel called from heaven, ". . . Abraham, . . . Lay not thine hand upon the lad, neither do thou anything unto him; for now I know that thou fearest God, seeing thou hast not withheld thy son, thine only son from me."

Abraham must have known what a great sacrifice our Father in heaven made when he sent his Son to the earth. Jesus Christ was sent to the earth, was killed, and was resurrected that all men might be resurrected.

Abraham was obedient and had great faith in our Heavenly Father. Abraham was blessed for his faithfulness.

JOSEPH

from the Bible, Genesis Chapter 46

Joseph was sold into slavery by his jealous brothers. In Egypt, Joseph understood the meaning of the king's dreams. The king was so pleased that he made Joseph the governor of the land. Joseph had come to Egypt as a slave and later became the second most powerful man in the country.

During a famine, Joseph's brothers came to Egypt for grain. Joseph gave it to them, but they didn't know him. Sometime later Joseph told them who he was. He asked his father and all of his family to come to Egypt to live. Jacob, Joseph's father, was very happy when they met again in Egypt, for he had thought Joseph was dead.

Joseph was kind to the brothers who had meant to do him harm.

THE BABY MOSES
from the Bible, Exodus Chapter 2

The Hebrew slaves were becoming such a great nation in Egypt that the king was afraid the slaves would overpower their masters. He ordered that all little Hebrew boys be killed when they were born.

A Hebrew woman wanted to save her child, so she placed her baby in a little boat in the river. The baby's sister watched to see that no harm would come to the baby.

The king's daughter came to the river to bathe. She found the baby and decided to take care of him. She hired a Hebrew woman to be his nurse, not knowing that she was the baby's real mother.

The baby was adopted by the king's daughter and he was treated as her own son. She called him Moses.

As a man, he was a leader of his people. He led his people out of Egypt so they wouldn't be slaves any more. Moses was one of the great prophets of the Lord.

MOSES THE DELIVERER
from the Bible, Exodus Chapter 2

Moses was a great prophet, lawgiver, and deliverer of the children of Israel. He was also a messenger. He was a messenger between God and his people. During the years of wandering in the wilderness, God led the Israelites through Moses.

When the Israelites left Egypt, they were guided by a great cloud in the day and at night there was a pillar of fire.

They were camped by the Red Sea when their scouts saw the Egyptian army coming in the distance. With the sea on one side and the enemy on the other, the people began to panic.

Moses stretched out his hand and the waters parted, letting the children of Israel cross on dry ground. They escaped from the Egyptians who wanted to put them under slavery again. God helped the Israelites through Moses.

THOU SHALT HAVE NO OTHER GODS BEFORE ME
from the Bible, Exodus 20:1-3

The Lord said that we should have no other gods before him. This means that nothing should be loved more than God.

Sometimes Mother asks me which I would like for dinner—pie or cake. If I answer pie, I am saying that I like pie better than cake. I am putting pie before cake.

Sometimes we have to choose between God and other things we like. Some people like to play more than to worship God, so they stay home from church. They are putting play before God. Some like money more than God, so they keep their tithing instead of giving God what is rightfully his. They are making money more important than God. We who love God more than anything else know that we must not put what we want before what God wants. We do what God wants us to do. We put nothing before that.

The Lord says that we should have no other gods before him.

THOU SHALT NOT MAKE UNTO THEE ANY GRAVEN IMAGE

from the Bible, Exodus 20:4-5

The Lord says that we should not make any wood or stone images to worship. These images are something like dolls or statues. Long ago the people made these images and prayed to them, thinking that the image could answer their prayers.

We know that we should pray only to our Father in heaven and not trust in things of wood or stone. The God that we believe in and worship is truly our Heavenly Father. He loves us. He hears our prayers and will help us.

It is important that we always trust our Heavenly Father and not make unto us any graven image.

THOU SHALT NOT TAKE THE NAME OF THE LORD THY GOD IN VAIN

from the Bible, Exodus 20:7

    The Lord says that we should not use his name carelessly. It should *never* be used as a swear word. Our food, clothing, homes, and all in the earth are given us by our God. Even our lives are given us by our Father in heaven. One way we can show our thanks to our God for all these things is to use his name reverently. We use his name lovingly and kindly. He is God! His name is holy.

    I pray that we may never take the name of the Lord our God in vain but always use it reverently.

REMEMBER THE SABBATH DAY, TO KEEP IT HOLY

from the Bible, Exodus 20:8-10

The Lord says that we should not work on Sunday, but that we should keep it holy. The Sabbath day was blessed and made a holy day of rest. He says that we should do our work in six days. We will be happier if we have one day to rest from our work. This is the way God planned it. He knew it would be for our good. Sunday is a special day to think and learn about our Heavenly Father. We should go to church and sing and pray and worship God. We should always remember the Sabbath day and keep it holy.

HONOR THY FATHER AND THY MOTHER

from the Bible, Exodus 20:12

The Lord says that we should honor our fathers and mothers. This is as it should be.

If the owner of a store gave you all the things in his store, I'm sure you would appreciate it. You would thank him many times and honor him in all the ways you could. Your parents buy "a store full" of things for you in your life time. They do more than this. Have you ever cared for a small baby? If you have you know that they take a lot of care. Parents care for their children in many ways. For years before you can understand and say "thank you," they give you love and care.

When you get older you start helping your parents all you can. Children do what their parents ask. This is one way children can honor their fathers and mothers. Families work together, for they love one another. Parents sometimes make mistakes, but children know that their parents are wiser than they are.

We appreciate all our parents do for us. We love and trust our parents. We honor our father and mother, for this makes us happy.

THOU SHALT NOT KILL
from the Bible, Exodus 20:13

The Lord tells us that we should not kill. Only God can create life. We cannot make a seed, an insect, or a bird. Life is very precious. If we take it away—we cannot give it back.

We are all the children of our Heavenly Father. He wants us to help take care of each other. We cannot be happy if we are afraid that someone will hurt us or take the life of our loved ones. God wants all his children to be happy.

Life is a gift of God. It is sacred. No one has the right to take it from another.

THOU SHALT NOT STEAL

from the Bible, Exodus 20:15

The Lord tells us that we should not steal. This means that we should not take what does not belong to us.

We want our belongings to be safe. We don't want to worry about their being taken from us. We cannot be happy if we take from others what belongs to them. Our Father in heaven knows that we will be happier if we work for the things we want. We will care for them better and appreciate them more if we know how hard we must work for the things we use.

Our Heavenly Father would like us to share with others who don't have as much as we. No one should have to take what he really needs. If we all learn to share and work together, we will all be happy.

THOU SHALT NOT BEAR FALSE WITNESS AGAINST THY NEIGHBOR

from the Bible, Exodus 20:16

The Lord has told us that we must not bear false witness against our neighbor. This means that we should not tell lies about people.

We cannot be happy if we make others unhappy. If we say someone has done something bad when he hasn't, it will surely make him sad. It is not being honest. We don't want anyone to blame us for something he or someone else has done. This is not right, just as it is not right for us to hurt someone by telling a lie. We should always be honest with ourselves and those around us.

THOU SHALT NOT COVET

from the Bible, Exodus 20:17

The Lord tells us that we should not covet. To covet is to want very badly something that belongs to someone else. It is to be jealous of other people because they have something that we would like. We cannot be happy if we are greedy and envy others because of what they own.

If we covet what belongs to others, it may lead us to break another commandment which says we should not steal. We should work hard and plan wisely to earn the things we have need for. We will always be happier if we live the commandments of our Heavenly Father.

THE ISRAELITES' LACK OF FAITH

from the Bible, Exodus 32

The Israelites' lack of faith was a great problem to Moses while he was their leader. Quickly did they forget the special help and care that God had given them. They often rebelled against Moses.

During Moses' absence while he was on Mount Sinai, they became discouraged and asked Aaron to make an idol to be worshiped in place of Jehovah. Aaron gave in and had a golden calf made.

When Moses returned from the mount with the tablets of the commandments, he saw his people worshiping a golden idol. Moses was angry as well as shocked when he saw the golden calf. He threw the tablets down and broke them.

The Lord was very angry, for the people had made an idol. They sinned against the Lord because of their lack of faith.

SHADRACH, MESHACH, AND ABED-NEGO

from the Bible, Daniel 3:1-30

A long time ago, three men would not worship a statue of a king. They were put in a very hot furnace. An angel kept them from harm. God saved them because they believed in him.

We should worship only the true God.

DANIEL IN THE LIONS' DEN

from the Bible, Daniel 6

Daniel knew that the king had made a new law. The law said that no one could pray to his God. Daniel always prayed to God. Even with this new law, he still prayed to God. Daniel was faithful. He opened his windows and prayed three times a day.

Daniel's enemies took him to the king. The king liked Daniel, but he could not change the bad law. Daniel was put in a den of hungry lions.

The next morning the king went to the den. Daniel was not hurt. God had sent an angel to close the lions' mouths.

The king was happy that Daniel was not hurt. He knew that God had saved him. God will watch over us if we are faithful.

I THINK WHEN I READ THAT SWEET STORY

by Jemima Luke

I think when I read that sweet story of old,
When Jesus was here among men,
How he called little children like lambs to his fold,
I should like to have been with him then.

I wish that his hands had been placed on my head,
That his arms had been thrown around me,
That I might have seen, his kind look when he said,
"Let the little ones come unto me."

Yet still to his footstool in prayer I may go,
And ask for a share in his love;
And if I thus earnestly seek him below,
I shall see him and hear him above.

Reprinted by permission of the Corporation of the President of the Church of Jesus Christ of Latter-day Saints.

JESUS AMONG THE DOCTORS IN THE TEMPLE

from the Bible, Luke 2

When Jesus was twelve years old, he went with his mother and Joseph to the temple in Jerusalem to celebrate the Passover.

After the celebration, Mary and Joseph started home. Sometime afterward, they discovered that Jesus was not with the group, as they had thought. They hurried back to Jerusalem to look for him. It took three days for them to find him. He was in the temple with the doctors who were teachers of the Law. The men were amazed at the wisdom and understanding of the young boy.

Mary asked Jesus why he would cause them so much worry. Jesus said, "How is it that ye sought (looked for) me? wist (would) ye not that I must be about my Father's business?"

THE BAPTISM OF JESUS

from the Bible, Matthew 3:11-17;

Mark 1:9-11

Jesus went to John the Baptist and asked John to baptize him. John didn't think that he was worthy to baptize Jesus, the Son of God. Jesus knew that it was necessary that John baptize him. So Jesus was baptized. He showed us the way.

A voice from heaven said, "This is my beloved Son, in whom I am well pleased."

Our Father in heaven is pleased when we are baptized.

JESUS STOPPED THE STORM

from the Bible, Matthew 8:23-27

Jesus and his disciples went onto a ship. A great storm came. Jesus was asleep. His disciples came and woke him. They were afraid that they would die in the storm. Jesus asked why they were afraid. He said they didn't have enough faith. Then he told the winds and sea to be still. The storm stopped. The disciples were surprised that the winds and sea would obey him.

JESUS HEALS THE BLIND

from the Bible, Matthew 9:27-31

Two blind men came to Jesus and asked him to have mercy on them. Jesus asked them if they believed that he was able to heal them. They said, "Yes, Lord."

Then he touched their eyes and told them it would be as they believed. They did have faith that he could heal them, for they were healed.

FAITH

from the Bible, Matthew 14:25-33

One night the disciples of Jesus were out on a lake in a boat. They saw Jesus walking to them on the water. The disciples were afraid, for they thought it was a spirit. Jesus told them not to be afraid that it was he.

Peter said, "If it is you, let me come to you on the water."

Jesus said, "Come."

Peter started walking on the water to Jesus. But when he saw the high waves he became afraid and began to sink.

Jesus put out his hand and saved Peter. He asked Peter why he had so little faith, why did he doubt?

We could do many things if we had enough faith. Most of us are like Peter. We have too little faith, and we doubt.

THE TEMPTATION OF JESUS

from the Bible, Matthew 4:1-11

Jesus went into the wilderness. He went without food for forty days and forty nights. The devil came and tempted him. He said, "If thou be the Son of God, command that these stones be made bread."

Jesus didn't do as the devil said because he knew that man does not live by bread alone. He knew that he would make his Spirit stronger by not letting the body always have what it wanted.

The devil promised to give Jesus all the kingdoms of the earth if he would worship him. Jesus wouldn't worship the devil, for he knew he should worship only our Father in heaven.

I pray that we will not be tempted to serve the devil but always worship our Father in heaven.

LET THE LITTLE CHILDREN COME

from the Bible, Mark 10:14-16

Jesus loved little children. He said, "Suffer (let) the little children to come unto me, . . . for of such is the kingdom of God." He took them up in his arms, put his hands upon them, and blessed them.

I hope I can live so that I can go to live with Jesus in his heavenly kingdom.

THE GOOD SAMARITAN

from the Bible, Luke 10:29-37

While traveling, a man was robbed and beaten by thieves. He lay there waiting for help. A man saw him but passed by. Then another man came by, but he didn't help. Later, a Samaritan came and saw him. He felt sorry for the wounded man and helped him.

Jesus said that we should help those who need help. If we do, we shall be good neighbors.

FEEDING THE 5000

from the Bible, John 6:1-13;

Matthew 14:15-21

A great many people followed Jesus because they wanted to hear his stories and see the miracles he performed.

One evening when it began to get late, the disciples wanted Jesus to send the people away. Jesus didn't want to send them away as he knew they were hungry. He asked how much food there was. One of the disciples, Andrew, said, "There is a boy here, who has five loaves of bread and two small fish."

Jesus asked the people to sit on the grass in groups of fifty. There were about 5000 people.

Then Jesus took the bread and fish and blessed and broke them. The disciples passed the food to the people. When they had all they wanted, the disciples gathered up the food. Twelve baskets of food were left.

The people knew that they had seen a miracle. They wanted to make Jesus their king, so he slipped off alone and went into a mountain. Jesus wanted them to believe in his heavenly kingdom or the kingdom of God. They wanted an earthly kingdom where he would make life easy for them.

The Church

GOING TO CHURCH

Our Heavenly Father wants us to go to Sunday School, Primary, and Sacrament meeting. He wants us to think of him while we are in his house. He will be happy if we listen and remember the things our teachers tell us.

TEN COMMANDMENTS OF REVERENCE

by May Spencer

1. Thou shalt strive with all thy might to get to Sunday School on time.
2. Thou shalt go quietly to thy seat and not push or shove, for there is room for all in the house of the Lord.
3. Thou shalt not disturb thy neighbor by whispering, for he has come to get the best he can.
4. Remembering that thou art in the house of the Lord, and it is thy duty to keep it holy.
5. Honor thy officers and teachers that thou mayest learn the things they have come to teach thee, that thou mayest grow strong in the sight of the Lord.
6. Thou shalt not laugh at the most humble of prayers, for "Prayer is the soul's sincere desire."
7. Thou shalt not refuse to take part in any work of the Church, for by thy work shalt thou be known.

8. Thou shalt use the time during the Sacrament service to think of the Savior and the life he gave for us.

9. Thou shalt not criticize nor covet thy neighbor's clothes.

10. Thou shalt not go home without thanking the Lord for the blessings thou hast received in the Sunday School.

Used by permission of *The Instructor*.

THE GOLDEN PLATES

by Rose Thomas Graham

The golden plates lay hidden
Deep in a mountainside,
Until God found one faithful,
In whom he could confide.

A record made by Nephi,
A Godly man of old,
Now, in the Book of Mormon,
The story is retold.

Reprinted by permission of the Corporation of the President of the Church of Jesus Christ of Latter-day Saints, copyright owner.

AN ANGEL CAME

by Rose Thomas Graham

An angel came and spoke to man
About the everlasting plan,
That God would send again to earth
The same as at the Savior's birth.

Our prophet Joseph was the one
God chose, and with his holy Son,
Told him the things that he must do
To bring the truth to me and you.

So children grown, and children small
It is God's hope that one and all
Will listen, learn, and work and pray,
To follow this, the only way.

Reprinted by permission of the Corporation of the President of the Church of Jesus Christ of Latter-day Saints.

THE PROPHET JOSEPH SMITH

It was through Joseph Smith that the Church of Jesus Christ was restored. He lived from 1805 to 1844. In Palmyra, New York, he was told in a vision of some ancient records. When in 1827 he received these tablets with sacred writing, he translated them into the Book of Mormon.

The Church was organized in 1830. As prophet and seer, he led the Church until he and his brother were murdered by a mob at Carthage, Illinois, on June 27, 1844.

He was a prophet of God. He prophesied the Civil War nearly thirty years before it happened. His other prophecies occurred as he said. He was the most important person to live in the world since Jesus Christ. Joseph Smith was truly a prophet of God.

THE RESTORED CHURCH OF JESUS CHRIST

When Jesus Christ was on the earth, he set up his Church. Then he was killed by the wicked people.

Because of wickedness, the gospel was taken away. The Church of Jesus Christ was no longer here on the earth.

This Church was restored through the Prophet Joseph Smith. This was the greatest thing that has happened to this earth since the resurrection of Jesus Christ. Jesus himself gave Joseph Smith the power to reorganize The Church of Jesus Christ of Latter-day Saints.

When we are baptized, we become members of this Church.

"Except a man be born of water and of the spirit, he cannot enter into the kingdom of God."*

John the Baptist baptized Jesus Christ, and John gave the power to baptize to Joseph Smith.

---

*John 3:5.

The Church of Jesus Christ of Latter-day Saints is the true Church of Jesus Christ because it was given by Jesus himself.

THE CHURCH OF JESUS CHRIST OF LATTER-DAY SAINTS

The Church of Jesus Christ of Latter-day Saints was founded in 1830 in New York by Joseph Smith.

The beliefs are based on the four standard works: the Bible, the Book of Mormon, the Doctrine and Covenants, and the Pearl of Great Price.

The Book of Mormon is a history of ancient people who lived here on this, the American continent. The Doctrine and Covenants is a book of revelations, and the Pearl of Great Price consists of writings of Moses and Abraham.

The Church is organized with a presidency. The President is prophet, seer, and revelator. There are Twelve Apostles. Other officers are: patriarchs, seventies, high priests, elders, priests, teachers, and deacons.

A group of about 500 members are organized into a ward. The bishop and his counselors oversee the ward. Five to ten wards are grouped into a stake. The stake presidency is responsible for the stake. Nearly 400 stakes and 75 missions are organized in the Church.

There are now over 2 million members of this restored Church of Jesus Christ.

OUR PROPHET

We love our prophet for the beautiful lessons he has taught us and is teaching us day by day. We know he is a prophet of God here on earth.

Our Heavenly Father isn't here on the earth, so he has his prophet speak for him. Our prophet tells us the things our Heavenly Father wants us to know.

We love our prophet and love to do as he asks. We pray for him and are loyal to him. He will lead us in the right paths.

THE KINGDOM OF GOD

It takes three things to make a fire: fuel, air (oxygen), and heat. Leave out any one of them, and a fire cannot burn.

This is as it is with the kingdom of God. It takes, faith, repentance, and baptism. Leave out any one of them, and you may not enter the kingdom of God.

HOW TO GET TO HEAVEN

One of the Russian spacemen who doesn't believe in God made fun of people who do. He said that he didn't "see heaven" while he was in outer space. We know that he wouldn't possibly see heaven when he didn't even believe in God.

A long time ago some people believed that heaven was just above the earth. They were wicked people. They decided to build a tower "whose top may reach unto heaven."* Perhaps they thought that they could get to heaven that way. The Lord knew that this proud and wicked people would have to become more humble. He caused their language to be mixed up.

When they could no longer understand and talk to each other, they lost interest in the tower and spread throughout all the earth. The Tower of Babel was never finished.

We know that they would never have reached heaven that way. Nor will anyone ever get to heaven in a space ship.

The Lord has told us how we may get to heav-

---
*Genesis 11:1-9.

en. We must obey all the commandments of God. We can be sure that only those who live the commandments of God will ever see heaven.

("Heaven" in this story refers to exaltation in the kingdom of God, which is the goal of all Latter-day Saints.)

The Gospel

REPENTANCE

(A little step or a big one)

It is possible to step across the Mississippi River if you go where it begins. The longer it gets, the bigger it becomes, and the harder it is to cross it.

That's the way it is with breaking a habit. When a bad habit is just beginning, it is easy to break. The longer it lasts, the harder it is to break it.

I hope we will break bad habits before they get to be big ones.

A ROAD MAP FOR LIFE

If you are going for a long trip, where you have never been before, you get a road map to show you the way. A map will help you so that you won't get lost.

Our life is like a trip. We have never been through this life before, so we don't know the way. The gospel is our road map. It tells us how to live so that we won't get lost. If we will follow the directions of the gospel, it will take us back to our Heavenly Father.

SIN AND FAITH

by Randon B. Maughan

If you don't brush your teeth, decay will soon destroy the tooth. First, the liquid called acid will go through the enamel. The enamel is the part of your tooth that you see. Next, the softer part which is called the dentine is attacked. Last of all, the pulp is attacked. When the acid reaches the pulp, you have a toothache, which doesn't feel very good. If you don't do something about it, you may lose your tooth.

The same thing happens when you let sin into your life. When you don't do something about it, you lose faith. Sin can very easily destroy your life. It will destroy your faith as decay will destroy your teeth. Keep sin out of your life everyday and you will not lose your faith.

BAPTISM

by Wallace F. Bennett

I like my birthdays ev'ry one.
Each brings a greater joy to me,
But I can't wait until I'm eight,
For then I'll be baptized, you see.

To be baptized as Jesus was
By one who holds the priesthood true,
And thus obey God's holy laws
Is just the thing I want to do.

When hands are laid upon my head
Then I'll receive the Holy Ghost
Because I'll do as Jesus said,
I'll get the blessing I want most.

Reprinted by permission of the Corporation of the President of the Church of Jesus Christ of Latter-day Saints.

I WANT TO BE BAPTIZED

by Teresa Maughan

I want to be baptized. This will mean that I will be a member of The Church of Jesus Christ of Latter-day Saints. Then I will be able to live with Heavenly Father some day. Jesus told us that we should be baptized. To show how important it is, he had John the Baptist baptize him. Jesus said that our sins will be forgiven. It is like being born again, for we start all over again.

I want to be confirmed a member of the Church and be given the Holy Ghost. The Holy Ghost will help guide me. It will help me know right from wrong. I want to be a good member of the Church of Jesus Christ.

It's my prayer that we may all live worthy to be baptized.

BAPTISM

Do you want to be baptized? I will tell you what you must do and what it means to be baptized.

First, you must have faith and repent from all wrongdoing. You must show by your actions that you really desire to live by the teachings of Christ.

When you are baptized, you become a member of the Church of Jesus Christ. This is the kingdom of God on the earth.

You go into the water as Christ was buried in the tomb. You come up from the water as he was resurrected from the tomb. The water also represents a cleansing of our sins.

When Jesus Christ was on the earth, he asked John to baptize him. Jesus set the example for us.

THE HOLY GHOST
(Do We Listen for the Buzzer?)

By Dean L. Maughan

Sometime ago some small children were in the mountains looking for some petrified wood. They had been told to listen and watch for rattlesnakes. As they walked near a sagebrush, they suddenly heard the buzz of a rattlesnake. The noise warned them not to come closer. They watched the snake flick its tongue in and out and then move away.

How many of us live so that when the buzzer of the Holy Ghost rings, we will hear it? Let us live the gospel so that we might hear the still small voice of the Holy Ghost.

THE HOLY GHOST

When you are confirmed, someone holding the authority puts his hands upon your head and says these words:

"By authority of the Melchizedek Priesthood, and in the name of Jesus Christ, we lay our hands upon your head and confirm you a member of The Church of Jesus Christ of Latter-day Saints, and say unto you, Receive the Holy Ghost."

This is the way you are made a member of the Church of Jesus Christ. You are also given the gift of the Holy Ghost.

If you live worthy so that the Holy Ghost will dwell with you, it will guide you in the right way.

PRAYER

Anonymous

Father of all, in heaven above,
We thank thee for thy love;
Our food, our home, and all we wear
Tell of thy loving care.

A PRAYER

Anonymous

Father, we thank thee for the night
And for the pleasant morning light
For rest and food and loving care,
And all that makes the world so fair.

Help us to do the things we should,
To be to others kind and good,
In all we do, in all we say,
To grow more loving every day.

PRAYER

Prayer is a way of talking to our Heavenly Father. We feel close to our kind Father when we talk with him in prayer. It is the way we thank him for all the many things he gives us.

Just as we talk with our father here on the earth, we can ask our Heavenly Father for the things we need. He loves all his children and wants to help us.

Our Heavenly Father likes us to come to him in prayer.

PRAYER ANSWERED

by Catherine Bowles

A family once had a cow that was very fond of apples. One day she came near choking to death with an apple in her throat. The father was away from home at the time, and the mother was ill, so there was no one except the children to do anything for the cow.

The children were crying because they were afraid that the cow would die. All at once the older brother thought he would pray. So with his younger brother and sister he asked the Lord to bless the cow and make her well. The children then went and looked at the cow, and sure enough she was well. While they were praying, a man had come and held the cow's head while another man removed the apple so she could get her breath and then she was all right.

Used by permission of *The Instructor*. (Adapted)

MY TITHING GIVES ME HAPPINESS

by Vilate Raile

My tithing gives me happiness,
I like to do my part,
It's one way I can show the Lord
I share with all my heart.

It gives me pleasure to return
This honest tenth to thee
It's very little when I count
All God has given me.

Reprinted by permission of the Corporation of the President of the Church of Jesus Christ of Latter-day Saints, copyright owner.

THE LAW OF TITHING AND JACOB

from the Bible, Genesis 28:10-22; 14:18-20

The law of tithing is not new. It was given to the ancient people long before Christ lived on the earth. The Bible tells a story about Jacob who was the son of Isaac and the grandson of Abraham.

Jacob slept by the side of the road one night while traveling to visit his uncle. As he slept, he dreamed of a great ladder that reached up to the heavens. Angels climbed up and down the ladder. The Lord appeared to Jacob in his dream. He promised to give all the land around to Jacob and his children. Jacob then promised to always serve the Lord and said, "Of all that thou shalt give me, I will surely give the tenth unto thee."

Jacob's grandfather also paid his tithing. Abraham paid his tithing to a high priest.

Blessings were given to Jacob and Abraham because they paid their tithing. We will be blessed if we obey this ancient law.

MY BODY

God gave this body to me. It is the home of my spirit, so I must keep it clean and strong.

The Word of Wisdom will help me keep my body clean, so my spirit will have a nice place to live.

OUR ENGINE—THE BODY

by Dean L. Maughan

An automobile engine will run on only one thing. Gas! Gasoline will make the engine go. If we put water in the engine, it will not run. It will not run if we put milk, fruit, or vegetables in the tank.

Our bodies are like the engine of a car. They will only work best when given the proper fuel. Our Father in heaven has said we must not use tea, coffee, or tobacco, or strong drinks in our bodies. If we do what our Heavenly Father tells us, we will have stronger bodies, and our engines will run better.

KEEPING THE WORD OF WISDOM

(This testimony was related by President George Albert Smith.)

When I was a child, I became very ill. The doctor said I had typhoid fever and should be in bed for at least three weeks. He told Mother to give me no solid food but to have me drink some coffee.

When he went away, I told Mother that I didn't want any coffee. I had been taught that the Word of Wisdom, given by the Lord to Joseph Smith, advised us not to use coffee.

Mother had brought three children into the world, and two had died. She was unusually anxious about me.

I asked her to send for Brother Hawks, one of our ward teachers. He was a worker at the foundry, and a poor and humble man of great faith in the Lord.

He came, administered to me, and blessed me that I might be healed.

When the doctor came next morning, I was playing outside with the other children. He was surprised. He examined me and discovered that my fever was gone and that I seemed to be well.

I was grateful to the Lord for my recovery. I was sure that he had healed me.

Used by permission of *The Instructor*.

MY BODY IS A TEMPLE

by Esther H. Doolittle

My body is a temple
That needs the greatest care;
It must be clean and wholesome
To house my spirit there.
And if I keep the temple,
My body, strong and clean,
My mind must be as wholesome,
Although it can't be seen.

My thoughts must be unselfish;
My words must comfort give;
My deeds must all be worthy
As long as I shall live.
The bracing air I breathe in,
The ocean where I swim,
The sports that build my muscle
I'll use for love of Him.

Reprinted by permission of the Corporation of the President of the Church of Jesus Christ of Latter-day Saints.

DO NOT BE DECEIVED

The catbird mews like a cat. It sounds like a cat, but it isn't one. It can also sound like some other animals. It can deceive others by making different sounds. We must not let others deceive us when they give false sounds. The ads on the TV, radio, and newspapers tell us that tea, coffee, liquor, and tobacco are good for us. They are like the catbird. They are deceiving people. Our Heavenly Father does not deceive us. He loves us and tells us what is not good for us. We know that he wants to help us do what is good for us. We believe him when he says that we should not use tea, coffee, liquor, and tobacco. Don't be deceived by the false sounds.

FREEDOM IN THE CHURCH

We have all been given the chance to choose between right and wrong. No one will force us to do the will of God.

> "Know this, that every soul is free
> To choose his life and what he'll be;
> For this eternal truth is given,
> That God will force no man to heaven.
>
> He'll call, persuade, direct aright,
> And bless with wisdom, love, and light:
> In nameless ways be good and kind,
> But never force the human mind."*

Satan has and will continue to persuade people to choose the wrong. All are given the opportunity to accept the principles of the gospel. Those who don't have a chance to hear it here on the earth will have a chance in the spirit world.

When we choose, we are deciding what place we will have in the next life. No one can decide for us. Our parents, teachers, and leaders can

---
*William C. Gregg

teach us the principles of the gospel. They may set the correct example. They may urge us to live so as to be worthy, but our future depends upon each of us. We each have to decide to live the principles of the gospel or not. It's up to us to choose our life, and what we'll be.

Home and Family

FAMILY

Anonymous

My father and my mother
Are both so kind to me
That every day I'll show them
How helpful I can be.

(This poem would be for the youngest children assigned in the Junior Sunday School.)

FAMILY

Anonymous

For Mother's love
And Father's care,
For brothers strong
And sisters fair,

For love at home
And work and play,
Our Father, God!
We thank thee.

ONLY ONE MOTHER

by George Cooper

Hundreds of stars in the pretty sky,
    Hundreds of shells on the shore together,
Hundreds of birds that go singing by,
    Hundreds of lambs in the sunny weather.

Hundreds of dewdrops to greet the dawn,
    Hundreds of bees in the purple clover,
Hundreds of butterflies on the lawn,
    But only one mother the wide world over.

Reprinted from *Favorite Poems Old and New* by Helen Ferris; Doubleday and Co., Inc., Garden City, New York, 1957.

A HOME OF LOVING DEEDS

by Victor Hugo

A house is built of bricks and stones
Of sills and posts and piers,
But a home is built of loving deeds,
That stand a thousand years.

KIND ACTIONS

Author Unknown

Mother so loving and father so true,
Sister and brother and wee baby, too;
All love one another, and each does his part
To show by kind actions the love in his heart.

DO WHAT'S RIGHT

Author Unknown

Dear God, there are so many things
    I ought to do and be—
    But please now, make me do what's right
So Mother will be proud of me.

Praising God

JESUS, THE SON OF GOD

Jesus was the Son of God! I believe that Jesus was the Son of God although he lived here on the earth. He was like many other children. He learned about his Father in heaven from his mother here on earth. He was a little boy who played games. He helped Joseph and learned to work with wood.

When he was a grown-up man, he healed the sick, made the lame to walk, and the blind to see.

He was killed because he said that he was the Son of God. After three days he was resurrected. Jesus was able to rise from the tomb because he really was the Son of God.

THANKS TO OUR FATHER

by Robert Louis Stevenson

"Thanks to our Father we will sing
For he gives us everything."

FOR HEALTH AND FOOD

Ralph Waldo Emerson

"For health and food, for love and friends
For everything thy goodness sends,
Father in heaven we thank thee."

DEAR LORD

Anonymous

Dear Lord, for these three things I pray:
To know thee more clearly,
To love thee more dearly,
To follow thee more nearly,
Every day.

MY SOUL IS THINE

Author Unknown

I say this prayer with all my heart
    And all the faith in me
That thou will always guide me, God
    Wherever I may be.

That thou wilt walk beside me in
    The sunshine and the rain,
And nothing I may do or think
    Will ever be in vain.

I want to serve thee always as
    The great and honored guest,
And for the glory of thy name
    To give my humble best.

To thank thee for thy blessings, and
    To ask thee to forgive
The many faults that haunt me and
    The selfish way I live.

I want to give my soul to thee
    And with thy guiding light
To walk thy way each golden day
    And through the darkest night.

WE THANK THEE

Anonymous

For mother-love and father-care,
For brothers strong and sisters fair,
For love at home and here each day,
For guidance lest we go astray,
    Father in heaven, we thank thee.

For this new morning with its light,
For rest and shelter of the night,
For health and food, for love and friends,
For ev'rything his goodness sends,
    Father in heaven, we thank thee.

GOD OUR FATHER MADE THE NIGHT

Author Unknown

God our Father made the night,
Made the moon and stars so bright;
All the clouds so far away,
The shining sun and the golden day.

God our Father made the skies,
Bees and birds and butterflies;
Tiny flowers and trees that wave,
These lovely gifts our Father gave.

Reprinted by permission of the Corporation of the President of the Church of Jesus Christ of Latter-day Saints.

FATHER, WE THANK THEE FOR THE NIGHT

by Rebecca Weston

Father, we thank thee for the night,
And for the pleasant morning light,
For rest and food and loving care,
And all that makes the day so fair.

(For the younger children 4-6)

From *Song Stories* by Patty Hill. Clayton F. Summy Co. Used by permission. (Public Domain)

FATHER UP ABOVE

by Mabel Jones Gabbott

Oh, Father, look on us today,
And bless us with thy love.
In Jesus' name we humbly pray,
Oh, Father, up above.

(Children 4-6)

Reprinted by permission of the Corporation of the President of the Church of Jesus Christ of Latter-day Saints, copyright owner.

LOVING CARE

by Nellie Poorman

God has numbered in the sky
    all the stars that shine on high;
    worlds so great and sparrows small;
God is watching over all.

He remembers night and day
    ev'ry child at work or play;
He will teach you what to do;
God is watching over you.

From *"Tuning Up"* of *The World of Music series*. Used by permission of Ginn and Company, owner of the copyright.

GOD'S DAILY CARE

by Marie C. Turk

As I watch the rising sun,
When the day has just begun,
I am thinking of the love
That comes daily from above.

Father, turn thine ear to me,
Let me offer thanks to thee,
For thy wise and tender care
Of thy children everywhere.

Reprinted by permission of the Corporation of the President of the Church of Jesus Christ of Latter-day Saints, copyright owner.

JESUS IS OUR LOVING FRIEND

by Anna Johnson

Jesus is our loving friend,
He is always near.
He will hear us when we pray.
Every child is dear.

Reverently and sweetly now,
We our voices raise.
Jesus is our loving friend,
And we sing his praise.

(The first verse alone might be used by the very small child)

Reprinted by permission of the Corporation of the President of the Church of Jesus Christ of Latter-day Saints, copyright owner.

THANKS TO OUR FATHER

Author Unknown

Thanks to our Father we will bring,
For he gives us everything,
Eyes and ears and hands and feet,
Clothes to wear and food to eat.

Father, mother, baby small,
Heav'nly Father gives us all.
Thanks to our Father we will bring,
For he gives us everything.

Reprinted by permission of the Corporation of the President of the Church of Jesus Christ of Latter-day Saints, copyright owner.

FATHER, THOU WHO CAREST

Author Unknown

Father, thou who carest,
For smallest tiny flow'rs,
Thou teachest bees and squirrels,
To save for winter hours,
To thee, we little children,
Our loving thanks would bring.
For all thy loving kindness,
Of all thy goodness sing.

From *Song Stories*, by Patty Hill. Clayton F. Summy Co., Used by permission. (In public domain)

I THANK THEE, DEAR FATHER

by George Careless

I thank thee, dear Father in heaven above,
For thy goodness and mercy, thy kindness and love,
I thank thee for home, friends, and parents so dear,
And for every blessing that I enjoy here.

Help me to be good, kind, and gentle today,
And mind what my father and mother shall say;
In the dear name of Jesus, so loving and mild,
I ask thee to bless me and keep me thy child.

Reprinted by permission of the Corporation of the President of the Church of Jesus Christ of Latter-day Saints, copyright owner.

LITTLE THINGS

by Julia A. F. Carney

Little drops of water,
Little grains of sand,
Make the mighty ocean
And the pleasant land.

Little deeds of kindness,
Little words of love,
Make the earth an Eden
As the heaven above.

From *"Little Things"* by Julia A. F. Carney. Used by permission of Exposition Press, Inc. owner of the copyright.

Seasonal and Special Occasions

RESOLUTIONS

Author Unknown

January is the time
For resolutions new,
So I'll turn some pages over
And think what I should do;
To be a better neighbor,
To share more as I play,
To try a little harder
My parents to obey.

Used by permission of *The Instructor*.

EASTER

What does Easter mean to you? A new dress, an Easter basket with candy, or a picnic?

Easter should remind us of Christ's greatest gift to man. His gift was his life.

He gave his life that all men might live again after death. Through the gift of Jesus, all of us will some day be resurrected.

HE IS RISEN

Bible, Matthew 28:1-6

In the end of the sabbath, as it began to dawn toward the first day of the week, came Mary Magdalene and the other Mary to see the sepulchre.

And, behold, there was a great earthquake: for the angel of the Lord descended from heaven, and came and rolled back the stone from the door, and sat upon it.

His countenance was like lightning, and his raiment white as snow:

And for fear of him the keepers did shake, and became as dead men.

And the angel answered and said unto the women, Fear not ye: for I know that ye seek Jesus, which was crucified.

He is not here: for he is risen, as he said. Come, see the place where the Lord lay.

FOR THE BEAUTY OF THE EARTH

by Folliott S. Pierpoint

For the beauty of the earth,
For the beauty of the skies,
For the love which from our birth
Over and around us lies,
Lord of all, to thee we raise
This our hymn of grateful praise.

For the wonder of each hour
Of the day and of the night,
Hill and vale, and tree and flower,
Sun and moon and stars of light,
Lord of all, to thee we raise
This our hymn of grateful praise.

Reprinted by permission of the Corporation of the President of the Church of Jesus Christ of Latter-day Saints, copyright owner.

MOTHER'S DAY

by Stephen Fay

Mother dear, who keeps me safe from every harm,
What shall I do, her kindness to repay?
This I'll do, and do it with a loving heart,
Make every day a cheerful Mother's day.

Copyright, Summy-Birchard Company, Evanston, Illinois. All rights reserved. Used by permission.

MOTHER DEAR

By Maude Belnap Kimball

Mother dear, I love you so,
Your happy smiling face
Is such a joy to look at,
It makes home a lovely place.

Mother dear, I love you so,
Your lovely shining eyes
Are just like stars that twinkle
Way up in the bright blue skies.

Mother dear, I love you so,
I will try all day through
To please our Heavenly Father
I'm so glad he gave me you.

Reprinted by permission of the Corporation of the President of the Church of Jesus Christ of Latter-day Saints, copyright owner.

HONOR THY MOTHER

George Washington's home was near a big river. Every spring when the boats from England sailed up the river, George would sit and watch them and wish he could ride on them. He came to know one of the captains and talked with him about life on the ocean.

One day George told the captain that he would like to become a sailor. The captain said that if his mother and brother would give their consent, George might become a sailor on that very ship when it sailed away.

George hurried home. His brother, Lawrence, thought that the experience would be good for him. His mother said that George might go if he really wanted to.

The day the ship was to sail George and his mother went down to the dock together. George's trunk had been carried on board, and he was very excited and happy.

When he went to say good-bye to his mother, he saw tears in her eyes. George quickly said,

"Mother, I am not going away. I can see that it will make you unhappy."

George had his trunk taken off the ship and went home with his mother. Her happiness meant more to him than his own wishes.

From "Behold Thy Mother," by Mothers' Day Program Committee for 1956, March 1956, p. 87. Used by permission of *The Instructor*.

FATHER'S DAY

My dad is my very best friend. He helps me in many ways. He teaches me to be honest and how to live as a "Mormon Boy" should.

I'm proud to be his son, and I want to help him every day. But the best way I can please him is to be the best boy that I can. I want to grow up to be just like my dad, 'cause he's the nicest man I know.

A SONG OF THANKS

by Mrs. E. Rutter Leatham

"Thank thee!" for the world so sweet;
"Thank thee!" for the food we eat;
"Thank thee!" for the birds that sing;
"Thank thee!" God, for everything!

Reproduced by permission of the American Book Company, from *First Year Music* by Hollis Dann.

THANKSGIVING

Ilo Orleans

We thank thee, Father,
God of all,
For green of spring
And gold of fall.

For woods and hills
And lakes and streams;
For laughter, song,
And hopes and dreams.

For music of
The sky and sea;
For love of friend
And family.

For shining stars,
For calm of night,
For cleansing rain,
For heaven's light.

For Mother's tender,
Loving care;
For things of beauty
Everywhere.

We thank thee for
The joy of living,
And sing a hymn
Of our Thanksgiving.

Used by permission of Mrs. Frieda K. Orleans, Executrix, Estate of Ilo Orleans.

MY GIFT

by Christina Rossetti

What can I give him
Poor as I am;
If I were a shepherd,
I would give him a lamb.
If I were a wise man,
I would do my part.
But what can I give him?
I will give my heart.

Public domain.

CHRISTMAS NIGHT

Author Unknown

Once within a lowly stable,
    Where the sheep and oxen lay,
A loving mother laid her baby,
    In a manger filled with hay.

Mary was the mother there,
    And Christ that baby fair.

God sent us this loving baby
    From his home in heaven above,
He came down to show all people,
    How to help and how to love.

This is why the angels bright,
    Sang for joy that Christmas night.

From *Song Stories* by Patty Hill. Used by permission of Clayton F. Summy Co., Illinois.

THE BIRTH OF CHRIST

The Bible, Luke 2:17

And it came to pass in those days, that there went out a decree from Caesar Augustus, that all the world should be taxed.

(And this taxing was first made when Cyrenius was governor of Syria.)

And all went to be taxed, everyone into his own city.

And Joseph also went up from Galilee, out of the city of Nazareth, into Judea, unto the city of David, which is called Bethlehem;(because he was of the house and lineage of David:)

To be taxed with Mary his espoused wife, being great with child.

And so it was, that, while they were there, the days were accomplished that she should be delivered.

And she brought forth her firstborn son, and wrapped him in swaddling clothes, and laid him in a manger; because there was no room for them in the inn.

TIDINGS OF GREAT JOY

The Bible, Luke 2:8-14

And there were in the same country shepherds abiding in the field, keeping watch over their flock by night.

And, lo, the angel of the Lord came upon them and the glory of the Lord shone round about them and they were sore afraid.

And the angel said unto them, Fear not: for, behold, I bring you tidings of great joy, which shall be to all people.

For unto you is born this day in the city of David a saviour, which is Christ the Lord.

And this shall be a sign unto you; ye shall find the babe wrapped in swaddling clothes, lying in a manger.

And suddenly there was with the angel a multitude of the heavenly host praising God, and saying,

Glory to God in the highest, and on earth peace, good will toward men.

THE WISE MEN

The Bible, Matthew 2:11

There were some wise men who lived in the east and studied the stars and heavens. When they saw a new bright star, they knew that the Son of God was born. They followed the star to Bethlehem. They wanted to see the Son of God and worship him.

The star was above the house where the baby lived. There "they saw the young child with Mary his mother, and fell down, and worshipped him: and when they had opened their treasures, they presented unto him gifts; . . ."

The wise men brought the gifts to thank our Heavenly Father for sending his Son to the world.

When we give gifts to each other at Christmas time we are remembering the gifts of the wise men. We can't give gifts to the Baby Jesus as the wise men did, so we give them to someone else that we love. Christmas is also a time to thank our Heavenly Father for sending his Son to the world.

Strength and Character

HONESTY

Write it down behind your ears.

This is the way people in a far away country (Czechoslovakia) say: Remember this!

I want to remember to always be honest so I will write it down behind my ears. I hope we will all remember to be honest. It will make us happy to be honest.

THE LONG AND SHORT OF IT

A giraffe and a mouse have the same number of bones in their necks. It all depends on what they do with them. So it is with us.

Everyone has 60 minutes to an hour, 24 hours in a day. What we do in life depends on what we do with the minutes, hours, and days. We should all use our time wisely and make the most of what we have.

DEAR GOD

Anonymous

Dear God,
Help me to use my eyes to see
Some bit of work
Waiting for me.
Help me to use my lips to say
A cheerful word
To make a glad day.
Help me to use my hands to do
Some kindly task
To show I love you.

SETTING A GOAL

One day I walked across a field that was covered with new snow. When I looked back at my tracks, I could see that I had wandered all about. I had wasted much time and many steps.

The next time I set my goal and walked toward it, never taking my eyes off. When I reached my goal, I looked back at my tracks. My tracks made a straight line to the goal.

In life we should set our goal and walk straight toward it.

HAPPINESS

by Mr. and Mrs. N. W. Christiansen

I am happy today for the sunshine,
For skies of gray or blue;
For within my heart is the song of life,
I'll live! I'll work! I'll do!

No cloud can cast a shadow,
Over courage such as mine;
And I'll sing my song as I go along,
I'll live! I'll work! I'll do!

Reprinted by permission of the Corporation of the President of the Church of Jesus Christ of Latter-day Saints, copyright owner.

HE DIDN'T GIVE UP

Thomas Edison didn't give up easily. After trying 8,000 unsuccessful ways to make a storage battery, he said cheerfully, "Well, at least we know 8,000 things that won't work. What we have to do now is to find the one way in which it can be done."

Because he didn't give up easily, he invented over a thousand different things. He changed the world and made it a better place to live.

I pray that we will try to make the world a better place, and that we will not give up easily when we find things difficult.

TRY, TRY AGAIN

By T. H. Palmer

'Tis a lesson you should heed,
    Try, try again;
If at first you don't succeed,
    Try, try again;
Then your courage should appear,
For, if you will persevere,
You will conquer, never fear;
    Try, try again.

FIGHT FOR THE RIGHT

Geronimo was the last Apache chief to surrender to the U. S. Army. It took 5,000 troops and 500 Indians to capture his band of 35 men.

He was fighting for what he thought was right. He believed that the white man was stealing the Indian's land. He was a fierce fighter.

We should fight for what we think is right. When others want us to break the Word of Wisdom or the Ten Commandments, we must be good fighters for the right. We must not surrender when we are on the Lord's side.

CHARTING A COURSE

Airplane and ship pilots use the stars to chart their course. By looking at the positions of the sun, moon, and stars, they know which way to go.

Our Heavenly Father helps us to "chart our course." He gives us prophets to lead us. He gives us the Bible, Book of Mormon, and other books to guide us. Our teachers help us to learn which way to go. If we are good pilots, we will chart our course so that we may go back to live with our Heavenly Father some day.

ROAD SIGNS

by Dean L. Maughan

All of us know what a stop sign looks like. It is a big sign with the word STOP on it. The stop sign is placed where one road meets another one. It is a danger point. It warns us that danger is ahead. Without the stop sign, something bad might happen.

As we grow up we will see many stop signs. We must stop and see whether the road is clear. Our parents and teachers tell us what many of these stop signs are. There is the stop sign that says we must not steal. There is a stop sign that says we must not tell a lie.

We must learn to obey the signs our parents and teachers tell us about. They will keep us from harm. I hope we will watch for the danger signs.

OBEDIENCE

Author Unknown

There is something that even a child can do,
That's greater than deeds of war,
It is only this—obey God's word,
For he can ask no more.

There is something that even a child can say,
That's greater than book or song,
It may be just this, I'll watch and pray,
That I may do no wrong.

OBEDIENCE

The first lesson that a mother black bear teaches her cub is to climb a tree when danger is near. The cub will not come down until its mother gives the signal that it is safe. If a cub bear learns to obey his mother, he may save his life.

If we learn to obey our mothers, we may save ourselves from harm. Obedience is the first law of the gospel. We must first learn to obey our parents; then we will be able to obey our Heavenly Father.

LITTLE LAMBS SO WHITE AND FAIR

Author Unknown

Little lambs so white and fair
Are the shepherd's constant care;
Now he leads their tender feet
Into pastures green and sweet.

Now they listen and obey,
Following where he leads the way;
Heav'nly Father, may we be
Thus obedient unto thee!

Reprinted by permission of the Corporation of the President of the Church of Jesus Christ of Latter-day Saints, copyright owner.

I HAVE TWO LITTLE HANDS

by Bertha A. Kleinmann

I have two little hands folded snugly and tight.
They are tiny and weak yet they know what is right.
During all the long hours till daylight is through,
There is plenty indeed for my two hands to do.

Kind Father, I thank thee for two little hands,
And ask thee to bless them till each understands
That children can only be happy all day,
When two little hands have learned how to obey.

Reprinted by permission of the Corporation of the President of the Church of Jesus Christ of Latter-day Saints, copyright owner.

GRAVITY

A 60 pound boy on the earth would weigh about 10 pounds if he were on the moon. This is because the earth has stronger gravity than the moon. Gravity has pull.

Doing what is right has "pull." The more we do what we should, the easier it is to keep on doing the right things. Doing wrong has its "pull." The more we do what is wrong, the easier it is to keep doing wrong.

We must choose which way we want to go, right or wrong. The right way is like the earth. It has stronger gravity or pull. It is easier to do right than wrong.

STUCK IN THE SAND

by Dean L. Maughan

Some Navajo Indians were busy digging sand from under their pick-up truck. You see, they were stuck in the sand. The wheels of the truck would only spin. By putting some canvas under the wheels it was quickly on the road again.

Sometimes we get stuck in the sands of life. Sometimes we get off the beaten road. A little smile, a kind push will soon put us on the road of the gospel again.

LET'S BE KIND TO ONE ANOTHER

by Evan Stephens

Let's be kind to one another,
Let us win each other's love,
Let each be a sister, brother,
As the angels are above.

Though we can't be pure and holy
While as mortals here we stay,
Yet we can shed love and kindness
'Round our pathway every day;

Yes, we should let love and kindness
Be our motto day by day.

Many hearts are sad and weary
Of the world with all its toil.
And this gloom, however, dreary,
Could be banished by a smile.

And that smile would cost you nothing,
Nothing more than would a frown;
One would raise them up to heaven,
While the other casts them down;

Let us then make earth a heaven
Turn to kindly smiles, our frown.

Reprinted by permission of the Corporation of the President of the Church of Jesus Christ of Latter-day Saints, copyright owner.

IT'S PLAIN THIEVERY!

by Constance Cameron

One day, when I was about eight, I was playing beside an open window while Mrs. Brown confided to my mother a serious problem concerning (about) her son. When Mrs. Brown had gone, my mother, realizing I had heard everything, said: "If Mrs. Brown had left her purse here today, would we give it to anyone else?"

"Of course not," I replied.

Mother continued: "Mrs. Brown left something more precious than her purse today. She left a story that could make many people unhappy. It is still hers, even though she left it here. So we shall not give it to anyone. Do you understand?"

I did. And I have understood ever since that a confidence or a bit of careless gossip which a friend has left at my house is his—not mine to give to anyone.

Reprinted from the November 1942 *Reader's Digest*, Copyright 1942 by the Reader's Digest Assn., Inc. Used by permission.

A HEALTHY SPIRIT

Why does your mother have you wash your hands before you eat? Because she wants you to be healthy. She doesn't want you to get germs into your food. Germs can make you sick. Sometimes you think you are clean. You look at your hands, and you can't see any germs, but they are there. Germs are too small to be seen, yet they can cause much trouble. That's why it's so important to keep clean.

There are other things that can hurt us, although they can't be seen. You may not see what will hurt you when you steal, tell lies, or swear. But these things are not clean. They are not good. They can cause trouble and make the spirit sick. Just as we must take good care of our body, so must we take good care of the spirit. We will have a healthy spirit if we live as our Heavenly Father tells us.

A NEW HOBBY

Many of us have hobbies. A hobby is something you do for the fun of it. Sometimes our hobbies are collecting things such as rocks, leaves, insects, buttons, dolls, coins, or maybe stamps.

Another hobby might be to collect good habits. Habits are things we do without thinking very much. Saying "Thank you" when someone gives you something or does something for you is a good habit. Saying "Please" is another good habit. To be honest, truthful, and trustworthy are good habits. Always being cheerful would be another good habit to add to the collection.

Maybe you will want to start the hobby of collecting good habits. It would be fun to see how many you can add to your collection. A hobby like this will surely make you happy.

THE LORD IS MY SHEPHERD

The Bible, Psalm 23

The Lord is my Shepherd; I shall not want.

He maketh me to lie down in green pastures; He leadeth me beside the still waters.

He restoreth my soul: he leadeth me in the paths of righteousness for his name's sake.

Yea, though I walk through the valley of the shadow of death, I will fear no evil: for thou art with me; thy rod and thy staff they comfort me.

Thou preparest a table before me in the presence of mine enemies; thou anointest my head with oil; my cup runneth over.

Surely goodness and mercy shall follow me all the days of my life: and I will dwell in the house of the Lord for ever.

INDEX

A

Aaron, 42
Abed-nego, 43
Abraham, 26, 88; faith and obedience of, 27-28; writings of, 67
Adam and Eve, 23
"An Angel Came," 63
Ark, 24

B

Baptism, 70, 79, 80; of Jesus, 47
"Baptism," 78
Beginning, In the, 23
Bennett, Wallace F., 78
Bible, 67, 88, 153
Blind, healing the, 49
Body, keep clean, 89, 164; like an engine, 90
Book of Mormon, 67, 153
Bowles, Catherine, 86

C

Cameron, Constance, 163
Careless, George, 121
Carney, Julia A. F., 122
Children, blessed by Jesus, 52
Children of Israel, 31
Christiansen, N. W., Mr. and Mrs., 149
Christmas, 141
"Christmas Night," 138
Church, Going to, 59
Church of Jesus Christ, restored, 65-66
Church of Jesus Christ of Latter-day Saints, freedom in the, 95-96; organized, 64, 67-68; to be a member of, 79, 82
Confidence, keeping a, 163
Cooper, George, 101
Course, charting a, 153
Covet, thou shalt not, 41

D

Daniel, and lions' den, 44
Dann, Hollis, 134
"Dear God," 147
"Dear Lord," 109
Deceiving people, 94
Devil, tempts Jesus, 51
"Do What's Right," 104
Doctrine and Covenants, 67
Doolittle, Esther H., 93

E

Easter, 126
Edison, Thomas, 150
Emerson, Ralph Waldo, 108
Exaltation, 72

F

Faith, 50, 70, 77, 80; lack of, 42
Faithfulness, of Abraham, 27-28; of Daniel, 44
False witness, 40
"Family," 99, 100
"Father, Thou Who Carest," 120
"Father, Up Above," 115
"Father, We Thank Thee for the Night," 114
Fathers, honor our, 36-37
"Father's Day" 133
Favorite Poems Old and New, 101
Fay, Stephen, 129
Feeding the 5000, 54-55
Ferris, Helen, 101
First parents, 23
First Year Music, 134
"For Health and Food," 108

"For the Beauty of the Earth," 128
Free agency, 95-96
Freedom, 95-96

G

Gabbott, Mabel Jones, 115
Germs, 164
Geronimo, 152
Goal, setting a, 148
God, 35; and Moses, 31; faithful to, 44; instructs Noah, 24-25; love of, 32; made the earth, 23; obey commandments of, 71-72; speak reverently of, 34; talked with Abraham, 26; will of, 95-96; worship, 33, 43
"God Our Father Made the Night," 113
"God's Daily Care," 117
Going to Church, 59
"Golden Plates, The," 62
Good Samaritan, 53
Graham, Rose Thomas, 62, 63
Gravity, 159
Gregg, William C., 95

H

Habits, break bad, 75; collect good, 165
"Happiness," 149
Heaven, 71-72
Heavenly Father, 23, 24-25, 27, 33, 39, 41, 69, 76, 79, 85, 90, 141, 153, 156, 164
He is risen, 127
Hill, Patty, 114, 120, 138
Hobbies, 165
Holy Ghost, given the, 79, 82; small voice of, 81
"Home of Loving Deeds, A" 102
Honesty, 40, 145
Hugo, Victor, 102

I

"I Have Two Little Hands," 158

"I Thank Thee, Dear Father," 121
"I Think When I Read That Sweet Story," 45
Idol, golden, 42
Images, graven, 33
Instructor, The, 61, 86, 91-92, 125, 132
Isaac, 27, 88
Israelites, 31; lack of faith, 42

J

Jacob, 88
Jealous, 41
Jesus Christ, 23, 27-28; baptism of, 47, 65, 79, 80; birth of, 139, 140; blessed little children, 52; faith in, 50; feeds the 5000, 54-55; heals the blind, 49; in the temple, 46; resurrection of, 127; Son of God, 107; stopped the storm, 48; temptation of, 51
"Jesus Is Our Loving Friend," 118
John the Baptist, 47, 65, 79
Johnson, Anna, 118
Joseph, in Egypt, 29

K

Kill, thou shalt not, 38
Kimball, Maude Belnap, 130
"Kind Actions," 103
Kindness, 29
Kingdom of God, 70
Kleinmann, Bertha A., 158

L

Ladder of Jacob, 88
Leatham, E. Rutter, Mrs., 134
"Let's Be Kind to One Another," 161-162
Lies, 40
Life, gift of God, 38, 126; road map for, 76; stuck in the sands of, 160
Lions' den, 44

"Little Lambs So White and Fair," 157
"Little Things," 122
Lord is my shepherd, 166
"Loving Care," 116
Luke, Jemima, 45

M

Mary and Joseph, 46, 139, 141
Maughan, Dean L., 81, 90, 154
Maughan, Randon B., 77
Maughan, Teresa, 79
Mishach, 43
Moses, as a baby, 30; returns with the tablets, 42; the deliverer, 31; writings of, 67
Mother, honor our, 36-37; honor thy, 131-132
"Mother Dear," 130
"Mother's Day," 129
"My Body Is a Temple," 93
"My Gift," 137
"My Soul Is Thine," 110-111
"My Tithing Gives Me Happiness," 87

N

Noah, 24-25

O

"Obedience," 155
Obedience, 156
"Only One Mother," 101
Orleans, Ilo, 135-136

P

Palmer, T. H., 151
Parents, honor our, 36-37
Passover, 46
Pearl of Great Price, 67
Perseverence, 150
Peter, faith of, 50
Pierpoint, Folliott S., 128
Poorman, Nellie, 116
Prayer, 85; answered, 86
"Prayer," 83
"Prayer, A," 84
Primary, 59
Prophet, of the Church, 69
Psalm, Twenty-third, 166
"Pull," 159

R

Raile, Vilate, 87
Rainbow, 24-25
Reader's Digest, 163
Repentance, 70, 75, 80
"Resolutions," 125
Resurrection, 127
Reverence, ten commandments of, 60-61
Right, do what is, 159; fight for, 152
Road signs, 154
Rossetti, Christina, 137

S

Sabbath day, keep holy, 35
Sacrifice, of Isaac, 27-28; of Jesus, 27-28
Sacrament meeting, 59
Samaritan, good, 53
Sand, stuck in the, 160
Satan, 95
Shadrach, 43
Signs, obey, 154
Sin, 77, 79
Smith, George Albert, 91-92
Smith, Joseph, 64, 65
"Song of Thanks, A," 134
Song Stories, 114, 120, 138
Spencer, May, 60
Spirit, a healthy, 164
Star, the, 141
Steal, 41; thou shalt not, 39
Stephens, Evan, 161-162
Stevenson, Robert Louis, 108
Sunday School, 59, 60

T

Ten Commandments, 42, 152; of reverence, 60-61
"Thanks to Our Father," 108
"Thanks to Our Father," 119
Thanksgiving, 135-136
Tithing, 87; law of, 88

Time, use wisely, 146
Tower of Babel, 71
"Try, Try Again," 151
"Tuning Up," 116
Turk, Marie C., 117

W

Washington, George, 131-132
"We Thank Thee," 112
Weston, Rebecca, 114
Wise Men, the, 141
Word of Wisdom, 89, 90, 94, 152; keeping the, 91-92
World of Music, The, 116